'LA CLARTÉ

NOTRE-DAME'

AND

'THE LAST BOOK
OF THE MADRIGALS'

SEAGULL
BOOKS
•
CELEBRATING
40 YEARS

THE SWISS LIST

Philippe Jaccottet

'LA CLARTÉ
NOTRE-DAME'

AND

'THE LAST BOOK
OF THE MADRIGALS'

Translated by John Taylor

LONDON NEW YORK CALCUTTA

www.bibliofrance.in

The work is published with the support of the Publication
Assistance Programmes of the Institut français

Seagull Books, 2022

Originally published in French as Philippe Jaccottet, *La Clarté
Notre-Dame* and *Le dernier livre de Madrigaux*

© Éditions Gallimard, Paris, 2021

First published in English translation by Seagull Books, 2022
English translation © John Taylor, 2022

Afterword: 'Leaning Back Against the Night'
© José-Flore Tappy, 2021

ISBN   978 1 8030 9 061 0

British Library Cataloguing-in-Publication Data
A catalogue record for this book is available from
the British Library.

Typeset by Seagull Books, Calcutta, India
Printed and bound in the USA by Integrated Books International

CONTENTS

La Clarté Notre-Dame

To José-Flore Tappy

I

Note dated 19 September 2012: 'This spring, don't forget the little vesper bell of La Clarté Notre-Dame, which sounds incredibly clear in the vast, grey, silent landscape—truly like a kind of speech, call or reminder, a pure, weightless, fragile, yet crystal-clear tinkling—in the grey distance of the air.'

(Indeed, *this*: I must keep it alive like a bird in the palm of my hand, preserved for a flight that is still possible if one is not too clumsy, or too weary, or if the distrust of words doesn't prevail over it.)

On a day perhaps at the end of winter (after checking it was 4th of March, thus about a year ago), while walking with friends and barely talking in a vast landscape heading down a gentle slope to a remote valley, under a grey sky, and it's another kind of greyness that predominates in such a season in these otherwise empty fields where no one is working yet, where we're the only ones walking, with no haste and no other goal than getting some fresh air. An ample, almost colourless space disturbed by no noise, to the extent that it could even seem sad, so deprived as it is of signs of life, of movements like those, for example, of a bird flying, which one would wish for, deep inside oneself. Moreover, although it was mid-afternoon, the very light, and even the word that would have designated it, seemed to be absent, whereas there was also no question of speaking of shadow, even less so of darkness.

A vast open, quiet space which had been appointed by who knows whom to represent silence, and better than that: something like a deep absence.

Up until then, nothing particularly strange, or that might have moved us. At best, perhaps, a kind of prelude to something we didn't know. Until the little vesper bell of La Clarté Notre-Dame Convent, which we still couldn't see at the bottom of the valley, began to ring far below us, at the heart of all this almost-dull greyness. I then said to myself, reacting in a way that was both intense and confusing (and so many times in similar moments I'd been forced to bring together the two epithets), that I'd never heard a tinkling—prolonged, almost persistent, repeated several times—as pure in its weightlessness, in its extreme fragility, as genuinely *crystalline* . . . Yet which I couldn't listen to as if it were a kind of speech —emerging from some mouth . . . A tinkling so crystalline that it seemed, as it appeared, oddly, almost tender . . . Ah, this was obviously something that resisted grasping, defied language, like so many other seeming messages from afar—and this frail tinkling lasted, persisted, truly like an appeal, or a reminder . . .

'The water troughs tinkle on the highest slopes of the mountains . . .'

I wrote this in my now-distant *Requiem* of 1946. And surely, the line didn't display great exactitude—a duty about which I was much less concerned back then than today. I still remember rather well which mountains they were (above Plans-sur-Bex, in the Vaudois Alps where I stayed as a teenager with an uncle, the owner of a very big historic chalet). On their 'highest slopes', there was not the slightest vegetation, thus no place for herds or troughs. If there was any tinkling at such an altitude, it could only have been, after some imaginative efforts, the sound of ice debris clinking together. But this matters little; commenting in 1990 on the reissue, to which I had finally consented, of this old and too ambitious poem, I wrote, however, something which was entirely truthful and which touches on what is essential: 'Formerly, I hardly liked mountains unless viewed from afar. In these past few years, I've rediscovered them, with my mind unburdened of all clichés and biases, and it's as if I were coming back, in this way, to a childhood region, to a part of childhood. Now I can accept without any further circumlocutions or hesitations that the tinkling of icy water falling into those troughs that resemble wooden boats anchored in the highest pastures sound to my ears as does a bell to the ears of a monk summoned to vespers or matins. I more than merely agree to this: I dream that this cold note guides me as far as possible into my heart.'

This is how, in my old age, while 'so few noises', so few signs of the world, still reach me, this bell—not a metaphorical bell this time—had again and unexpectedly spoken to me; and again, to orient me towards some summit whose name I would find on no map . . .

(Mountains . . . I'm thinking back today on what by far moved me the most during a recent stay in Sils-Maria: our excursion to Soglio, which until then had been a mere, yet nonetheless enchanting name in my mind because of what had been briefly written about it by Rilke, who sojourned there in 1919, and especially by Jouve, in his admirable narrative titled *Dans les années profondes*. And what was marvellous about those few hours that we spent there was that we were not disappointed—quite the opposite. The extraordinarily opulent meadows where the high grass couldn't conceal the multitude and diversity of the flowers; farther down, the chestnut woods sheltering small stone constructions which are still devoted today to storing chestnut harvests and which are posed there on the slope as, elsewhere, boulders would have been and, if we had been tempted to imagine, for as long a time. Finally, in what was much better than mere surroundings, instead almost a nest, or a cradle, the beautiful old village of Soglio, almost intact, with the surprise, in the centre, of the admirable Palazzo Salis, whose wing discreetly transformed into a hotel has still preserved Rilke's little room . . .

But especially, indeed especially, and this is why I have thought of recalling it here: across from us on the other side of the narrow Val Bregaglia, and visible above us, those intensely white mountains with particularly sharp teeth, a range that has always been called, unless I am mistaken, the Diavolezza—even as we have the Diablerets in the Vaudois Alps. One sees clearly why: for mountains are baleful, as some of Ramuz's most beautiful books recall. There's no use in revisiting this bad reputation. But no less founded is the sensation, which I experienced the day we were in Soglio, of an almost supernatural beauty crowned by this mountain range: a crown, indeed, the bristling of whose sharp points couldn't even be sensed as a threat in that they rise rather far above the thick prairies and the dense foliage, like a prolonged suspension of big white migrating birds; like, and I won't avoid saying this since the thought of devils had come to those who had long ago named the peaks in this way, a procession of angels whose wings would have stopped beating for ever . . .

In such ways, the most mercilessly real world sometimes compels us to invent unreal figures without whom we could not fully report on it.)

But I have wandered too far from my stroll beneath the March clouds, having been led off into a detour that is perhaps there only to postpone the effort that telling of the walk imposes and that runs the risk, at the same time, of making it vain.

I of course needed to place my hearing of this tinkling 'beneath the March clouds' among the surprises—in the final reckoning, quite a few—which have moved me in such deep, secret ways that today, when old age has aggravated my doubts of all kinds, I still cannot keep myself from seeing in these surprises some of those signs capable of almost making the doubts disappear.

And with this, all the same, I need to specify that it was a real, however humble, bell that had rung out there: I knew where it was, what it was used for. I could even imagine that when the sisters heard it, the few of them living in the convent with its beautiful name 'La Clarté Notre-Dame' had to leave, one a garden where she was breaking ground for a few spring sowings, others their book-binding workshop, or a cell in whose shelter, perhaps, the most aged among them had been resting for a moment, or meditating; similar to those small herds that a young shepherd tries to lead to the drinking trough before rounding them into their pen; except that here a few silent, obedient female lambs were seeking, deep inside themselves, to maintain, or increase even, their master's indulgence and purity . . .

The surprise of the vesper bell was thus by no means complete. Just as soon, I knew where to situate it, in the vast grey dwelling place that stood not very far from where we were walking. Should I henceforth have thought that its religious function, with the imagery that I have added here, would have affected the language that this function seemed to translate for me? In that I've remained respectful of the religious milieu, even if I haven't been immersed in it for a long time and, in the final reckoning, have never really been immersed in it, I have no reason to exclude the idea. (Which could appear in other people as a regret, or worse, as remorse; or simply a more or less vague nostalgia.) All the same, strangely or not: this religious resonance doesn't seem to have played the slightest role in the happy astonishment that was mine in that instant within the extensive, colourless landscape which, until then, had been so silent beneath a sky without breaches in the cloud cover and nonetheless threatless, this space about which there would almost be nothing to say except that it was vast, seemingly empty, peaceful and grey.

For this reason, against my preferences and because I knew the risks all too well, the obligation to use similes with 'like' and 'as if', a poet's tool that is almost too over-attentive and sometimes mechanical.

To be truthful, no comparison, as opposed to what sometimes happens, immediately imposed itself upon my mind. (Perhaps also because I doubted in advance that no comparison would satisfy me and exempt me from trying out others.)

So here I am, vaguely musing, for lack of something better, that a white bird would have flown across the landscape, as in Saint-Blaise back then, and illumined it in the same moving, incomprehensible way; but indeed not. I was too wide of the mark.

A breach which would unexpectedly have opened in the big grey clouds, letting a frail ray of light filter through as long as the tinkling of the bell lasted—

imagining this was perhaps a little less absurd, yet hardly less convincing.

I also needed to remember that it had been my hearing that had been affected, and yet in a discreet way that seemed tenderly persistent and perfectly tranquil. Not so far, in fact, from how one might have watched sleet enveloping the stroller for a few moments. Or also, because of the soft yet persistent sounds, so perfectly pure, so crystalline—but tender, let me insist on this, though I don't know how or why—I had to think of morning dew that would be—as in a fairy tale—winged, and metamorphosed into aerial sounds . . .

A limpidity which a heart would hardly be able to conceive, to hope for; and yet which would have enough power to act on a heart without any reference to its own nonetheless undeniable origin, as if only the word 'clarté', 'clarity', from the name of the place, La Clarté Notre-Dame, had been kept . . .

To my ear, the sound was also, if need be, a little like a kind of source suspended in the air . . . And this is therefore how, during these long years, all these 'encounters' have aroused in me initially a mute astonishment, and then, more deeply, in echo, a very special form of *joy*—even if this word now seems too strong to me; however, the feeling was not far from it —this is how these encounters seem to converge, like arrows to a target which, instead of being wounded by them, would be set ablaze . . .

Would thus my life, so close to the end, at last discover itself to be an appearance of sense as fragile, yet also as persistent as all those signs of which I would have been the gatherer, the 're-gatherer', and the too-clumsy interpreter?

In any event, this is the beautiful side of things, a favourable, flattering reading of my several books, and on them the light at once tender and pure such as, in this very moment, once more, I watch illumining the cradle of vegetation about to turn yellow, in imitation of the setting sun and, farther on, the sphinx already helmeted with the snow of Mount Ventoux, and higher up the great windowpane of the sky misted over by nothing.

Nothing mists it over . . . if not that which, in me, lives together with the light of the world in order to, one would say, destroy the light, to scorn it, to soil it, to turn it, not into night, which would be too beautiful, but into a lure that would make you vomit.

II

A few weeks ago, I watched and listened to on television a Belgian journalist—if this was indeed his job and his nationality, but this matters little—who, while imprisoned in Damascus for reasons of which I'm unaware and he himself was perhaps also unaware, had the rare chance of being liberated and, once back unscathed in Europe, of being able to tell the story of what, almost miraculously, had remained for him a merely sad misadventure. From his narrative, I'll probably always remember the brutal simple fact that, as he was going down a corridor which took him, as far as I can remember, from his cell to the office from which he would immerge a free man, he had heard, from each side of the corridor, the screams of those who were less lucky and who were being tortured. I immediately thought that I would never be able to chase this scene from my mind, and that it was of a kind that would sap everything that I had been able to, and still could, try to build to the glory of this earthly light that I had had the chance, unwarranted, surely unwarranted, to receive my share of, in this henceforth long life incredibly sheltered and, as a result, indeed little fashioned in a way on which could be founded thought that would also be valid for other lives.

The scene was all the graver in that I had heard, at some time before this, that the Syrian regime had dissimulated such ignominious places, such arenas for beasts more ferocious than those given this name, even under the site of those ruins of Palmyra where we had walked with my friends, eight years ago, with a sentiment of marvel which, moreover, I had preserved in the pages of a little book of which, I wonder now, I shouldn't be ashamed . . .

As if I needed to manage to think, *in extremis*, as to everything that I still experience in my enclave, my beautiful enclave protected who knows how or why from calamity, that beneath all the most admirable things that we have been able to contemplate in this world, there would be shadowy caverns in which would busy themselves diabolical beings such as privileged people of my sort would have glimpsed only in their worst nightmares; insignificant nightmares because they would always awake from them perfectly unscathed . . .

I write these lines today, 8 November 2012; outside my window, the trees, just beginning to turn yellow here and there, and the few clouds ever-changing yet bright like bundles of snow travelling in the vast sky, still remain as perfectly beautiful and peaceful, as if full of an unvoluntary goodness.

Once again this is, to the extent that it's becoming discouraging, and hopeless, the 'unequal combat' of my old poem from a half-century ago . . . As if I'd made absolutely no progress since then. At this moment when I should title these pages, instead—'Endgame'. Once again as well, a wave of weariness rolls over me, as if to spare me from acknowledging my inability to face up to this end.

So that every word written here on the page would be like one of those twigs with which Char had himself dreamt of building himself a rampart. Keep writing lines, as if tossing ropes onto the surface of an expanse of water, a minute pond or a sea extending as far as the eye can see, so that they will support some kind of safety net that will keep us from drowning. 'Life-saving poems' . . . Words, even any kind of word perhaps, to postpone the collapse, to make you believe that there would still be a chance of escaping unharmed . . .

(Thoughts that have come at night and partly faded away.)

. . . I rather often happen to wish that my life wouldn't continue indefinitely, since every month, if not every week, that goes by, aggravates the risk of adding a stone to the already sufficiently high pile from which a faceless, handless person will come to stone me to death . . .

. . . Without my having been granted the possibility of finding a way to counter this; nor of having understood anything about anything . . .

Even if one day I'd been able to consider from all angles all the greatest books of wisdom, I wouldn't have made any progress (but this would perhaps result from my natural laziness or my total incapacity to truly *think*). Therefore reduced, at the very end of my life's path, to staggering between two aspects of my experience, at least both of them being indubitable: the gathering of signs, which is almost all my poetry, with the last sign received, this year still, as the starting point of these pages—all those signs whose singularity is to be minute, fragile, barely graspable, evasive yet undoubtful, indeed quite the opposite: very intense; in the final reckoning, the most precious things that I will have received in my life, without my having looked or even hoped for them. And on the other hand, the growing fright of one who walks in a corridor of a prison in Syria and will never be able to efface from his mind the screams that he has heard rising from the lowest circles of Hell.

(During the same night, when the darkness deprives you, as so often, of your last allies, those companions delegated by the daylight and by everything that is more or less coloured by the sun, I also thought that only a kind of completely unsolemn tolling—one somewhat similar to rusty hinges creaking, a sound which the disappointed, frightened ear would seem to hear as only the word 'nothing' repeated with the nasty insistence of a henchman flaying his victim—could echo, at the end, the ungraspable and almost tender, prolonged appeal, on that already remote pre-spring day beneath a grey sky and in the great silent landscape where we were walking.)

. . . The screen of words raised 'to no longer see': and now from afar, over more than sixty years, the last line of my too ambitious, juvenile *Requiem* comes back to me: 'singing the glory of the earth to no longer see.' This was already to no longer see the horror of tortured hostages, and was the withdrawing movement of a young man of a little more than twenty years of age, totally spared by the war, in front of the same kind of horror; except that, more than sixty years later, he had become an old man also withdrawing, and doubtless, especially, in front of his own inevitable death . . .

And therefore, I would also say to myself: would you manage to make, as a screen against death, a fabric, a curtain, a screen composed of the poetically most admirable words; or—after all, this would be infinitely safer—would you borrow for this protective role one of the most beautiful poems ever written (and God knows that, having read so many, choosing one would be easy); or, seeking an even more effective protection, would you have the purest song that a musician has ever been able to produce raised in front of you as a shield? Well, *nothing would help*!

But now, all the same, on this first day of March, the light—widening, increasing, ascending—comes back to warm me near the window and is indubitably as *real* as the rise and growth of death in me. So that, once more, light seems to lead my hand, however weary it is now; and that, however vague, the memory of a moment of Sophocles' *Antigone* comes back to me—like so many other moments that would have the same sound and the same resonance—still another sort of tinkling in the inner sky?

In any event, this memory of an old man guided by a child, or a young woman, towards what could be his last refuge—this female figure could be called 'the light of my eyes'—is appropriate here, even if the guide is light itself: the faithful, silent and benevolent light.

'He who has entered the properties of age . . .'

It's the beginning of a poem in my old 'Livre des morts'—anterior to *Leçons*—when I was still far from being able to say this of myself; today, I should write instead: 'he who begins to enter the swamps of old age, its bogholes' . . . But at the same time, *outside*, what he sees getting readied, announced, in the garden and in the countryside, through the window which is not the one he would like to shut as well as possible, there is—in the very first rosy buds of an apricot tree and, farther on, in the very first rosy flowers of the almond tree, like a scattered dawn—the announcement, once more in his life, of an invasion of the world in his midst by swarms of minute, very frail angels, which a brief downpour or an unexpected gust would suffice to disperse into the grass or dirt. As if the plants had also received the gift of language, the gift of song, a song that could be translated only into beautiful liturgical Latin: EXSULTATE, JUBILATE, such as children could sing better than anyone . . .

Now, *now*: I must change the register, like the organist, the master of resounding avalanches, who grandly releases golden or silvery meteors, who goes to great lengths with his hand and feet to fill the church with other architectures inside the one in stone; who, by pulling on one or another of the wooden stop-knobs, releases his choice in turn—he is not unproud of his powers—of rumbling storms or crystalline chirping; like the organist (and I recall at this very moment the opening of Hölderlin's poem celebrating the birth of the Danube: 'As if from the splendid resounding organ / In the hallowed hall, on high'), I would need to play a lower, darker register . . . or worse, words foreign to any jubilation, incapable of any kind of harmony—if this were at last possible for me—because the window curtain masking the inevitable future would have been torn off, because the threshold of the beginning of the trial and judgement would have been crossed initially by almost imperceptible steps to the extent that one could still be deceived—and every word written here pushes it back, somehow . . .

(All the same, the song will have been sung, and nothing will be able to make it otherwise, a song ventured in a soft voice and even sometimes, indeed rarely, proclaimed at the top of the voice like an explosion of sunlight beneath the stone vaults.)

(17 March 2015)

(Despite everything.)

Getting up last night, I come across André Velter's radio show in tribute to Mahmoud Darwish, with some very beautiful readings, partly in Arabic, by his translator (and by himself?).

During which he says that if he wanted to write the words to a hymn for his (lost) homeland, he would do so by means of an almost impossible approach: *almond-tree flowers*.

As I went back upstairs to go to bed, seeing the two parallel beds with, under the sheets, the barely visible form of my sleeping wife—and as if inspired by Darwish's very breath, I seek to express these two neighbouring skiffs, heading down the current, obeying the imperious—secretly imperious—slope, in the same movement towards the ever-less-distant port . . . These two parallel skiffs, linked to each other, but whose sheets, whose linen, have for such a long time been uncrumpled, undisrupted by desire, even less so stained. Floating, heading down, sinking with no further word being spoken, but into a silence which no hostility enters—nor even, at that moment when I was moved by my reverie, no anguish, no despair; whereas there would certainly be good reason for it. These two skiffs joined without being so, irresistibly but calmly swept away by the current, the slope, the decline of time—in the middle of the almost even soothing night that unveils them for me. While nothing says what pitfalls await them, what torments that cannot be faced or eased, perhaps, before the port whose name rhymes without another one, 'mort'—less reassuring.

If I had a tribunal to face, as in the oldest fables (but there will be no tribunal, and I will be too *really* dead to face it), I would feel no fright, and my voice, my non-voice, would neither waver nor stutter, because I, too defenceless, would simply be *speechless*, as I have so often been in the past, among even the kindest friends, failing to have their certitudes or their self-assurance, feeling so clumsy, unsure, deeply, hopelessly ignorant.

Defenceless, however? Not completely, because I had experienced those unexpected encounters as by far the best part of my life, some of them remaining completely interior or almost, and of which I perceive today that they were all oriented in the same direction, embellished with a mute joy, directed towards what Plotinus, as a rereading of Shestov has just reminded me, called the Very High, with the same terms that Hölderlin, all the same, still dared to call the Sacred, and even the Gods. Encounters sometimes prepared, without my being aware of it, by all those fragments of poetry which had come to me from all sorts of places, which were so well engraved thereafter in my memory, and which also proceeded, however different they were, in the same direction.

To the extent that all the poems, as far back in time as one could reach, had for a single concern to become those signs of which Hölderlin rightly wrote that they 'help heaven'.

But not enough to have enabled this great multiple brightness to win out, over this ink that starts covering all of the still-open page to infest it from top to bottom.

(27 October 2016)

If I have put these pages away, kept them in reserve for such a long time, it's not because I reprove or only regret them. It's especially because they ended in a kind of result that wasn't one, since I couldn't do any better than to come up against ever-the-same metaphors, the same *translation* which, far from being fortified by its persistence, suffers from it; probably for failing to deeply convince me, to 'sway the decision, to carry conviction' (in accordance with a withdrawing movement that I've known only too well, for such a long time).

There's thus nothing surprising in my recalling of this old poem, 'The Unequal Combat', which dates back more than fifty years, with this disenchanted conclusion:

(It suffices to protect oneself with two reeds
    from the thunder,
When the order of the stars goes to rack and
    ruin on the water . . .)

It suffices to say that an entire lifetime has not given him a response; or perhaps worse: has aggravated the deep doubt.

As has been aggravated, since then, the 'thunder' whose rumbling nears, which would make not only real birds fly away and make even the bravest beasts lie low in their lairs, but also, one by one, all the signs that I've ever since applied myself to gathering with two flimsy reeds. However, all of a sudden, little suffices to completely devastate all the poetry that has nourished me ever since childhood; as if, at the end of my life's path, no word escaped the violence of what is much worse than a storm . . .

What is much worse? If not the short narration that still haunts me, made by the journalist who survived Bashar al-Assad's prisons and who, at the moment when he was freed, had walked hearing, around him, the moaning of the torture victims. I've never been able to put out of my mind those echoes rising from Hell. It could be, as I've said, that this had been produced in the underground prisons of Palmyra where, in 2004, before the disaster, I had, on the contrary, taken some enchanted footsteps. After that, how can one still believe in enchantments? How can one not see beneath them, including first of all those that will have irrigated my insignificant life so many times?

Now that I have arrived here, I should make a representation of an immense blankness on the page and inscribe it with a deadly silence; and withdraw, withdraw infinitely from this wall.

Having arrived at this too-old age, I have indeed had to imagine, even reluctantly, what the ceremony of my demise could be like, since skipping it, as our friend M. R. did, will only result in aggravating the sadness. For a long time, I still believed in the formulation that I had found in Cristina Campo's admirable poetry: 'Liturgy—like poetry—is gratuitous splendour, delicate wasting, more necessary than useful.' Even that eventually seemed no longer possible at all, to be a last, almost definitive lie. And moments of poetry that have long haunted me occurred to me.

In Hölderlin:

A riddle, what springs up purely

and in Claudel's *Tête d'Or*, a text bought in 1942 —and for a long time known by heart—this passage spoken by Cebes (while I have almost completely forgotten the rest of the play):

The chilly violet dawn
Slides across the distant plains, tinting each rut
    with its magic!

And in the silent farms the cocks crow:

Cock-a-doodle-doo!

It's the hour when the traveller, huddled up in
    his coach,

Awakes and, peering outside, coughs, and sighs.

And the souls newly born along the walls and
    woods,

Uttering feeble cries like little naked birds,

Fly away again, guided by meteors, into the
    regions of darkness.

—What time is it?

What was in those lines where Cebes speaks on the threshold of the death that he awaits? That he says this to *Tête d'Or* gives them a background of amorous friendship to which I should be sensitive, without even being aware of it. But the sensitive note was elsewhere: in those words of a traveller at the end of the night, the echo of which I would find much later in that haiku about crossing a barrier, my favourite haiku—which I translated:

Les voyageurs
demandent si la nuit est froide
avec des voix endormies

[The travellers
ask if the night is cold
with their sleepy voices]

They have gotten up before dawn, and it is perhaps to meet the sunrise that they have done so. Upon which I also recalled Goethe's 'Wandrers Nachtlied', which expresses the miracle of suspended time, of a moment of supreme peace, above everything, with the apprehension of a consoling or—one doesn't know—disquieting final rest. Footsteps are there as well and, in their halt, the glimpse of the *higher* to which these short poems are attached. And still in my sleeplessness, this traveller surprised in the quivering dawn, in his fragility, following birds, over the vast open space.

Suddenly, I found again these lines by Leopardi in his *Ricordanze* which had become over time a kind of password:

> In queste sale antiche,
> Al chiaror delle nevi . . .
>
> [In these ancient halls,
> brightened by snowlight . . .]

Why? It's probably a memory of the 'palazzo' in Recanati, on the rare occasions when it had snowed on the town that he sometimes hated. When the typical light of snowy days brightened, like a distant cold lamp, he recalls: 'these painted walls, those pictured herds', thus paintings or frescoes evoking an idyllic countryside in a well-preserved place, the luminous entering of the purest season, with a silent touch . . . And now this note from 1980, thus thirty-six years old, trying to understand the magic of the lines, evokes how the Italian has a 'silvery sonority—more or less how, so it seems to me, a believer should hear the little bell of the Elevation.' As if at almost twenty years of distance, the 'true' bell of the Elevation were making itself known: this is at least a rather nice proof of the continuity of my deep experiences.

Except that, at the sound of a bell, from the Far East as from our West, would come to mind numerous other, ever-moving quotations which would end up leading me back to the most admirable one, in which André du Bouchet and I unexpectedly came together, in the margins of one of Hölderlin's great poems:

> since
> for so little
> the bell used
> for ringing out
> dinnertime
> was out of tune, as if by the snow.

I cannot help but notice, at this very late moment, as I write these already trembling lines, that here I'm touching the exact heart of what made me write, and which excuses, or in any event explains and justifies, all my repetitions from the onset, or nearly so.

To which responds the little bell of my childhood, the one that my father would ring at the garden gate of my uncle's house in Geneva to announce our arrival, when we would go there from Moudon to celebrate New Year's Day with my cousins, a little bell tinkling shrilly in the falling snow . . .

(The winter sky, which weightlessly occupies two-thirds of my window, this morning of 6 December 2016, and which changes into silver threads the thinnest branches of the trees almost motionless below—it's almost as if once more the sky were encouraging me to celebrate its light . . . the illusion of light. As for he who gets immersed in listening to music, with closed eyes, and imagines himself, for as long as he listens, sheltered from the worst; while this coat protects him no better than that of the snow.

Comes the moment of the torn coat, the torn body, and too often tortures with no thinkable excuse for them.

Comes the destruction with no remedy and of which one cannot speak without lying, without flourishes, if not those armfuls of flowers that merely mask the unbearable.)

Post scriptum

(7 June 2020)

I've thought back on that day and told myself that if I had given up continuing, it was because I was already rather tired and that this fatigue had kept me from thinking of things related to that place, to that moment; which would have led me elsewhere and would have enabled me, perhaps, to not stop.

I perceived, for example, that I had neglected a detail that was not one. The territory of the convent sisters was to my right—while to my left there was, say, to simplify things, a profane countryside, and along that land, which was parallel to the convent gardens, there was a kind of stream walled by stones—if one wanted to follow it, it was almost a little dangerous, one could slip—and I told myself that this presence, in this place, on this day, of water flowing along the terrain should have alerted me . . . I should have thought of other things, and notably of the admirable ending of Dante's *Inferno*, where Dante and Virgil, at a given moment, rise towards the stars (specifically the last word of the poem, 'le stelle', which rhymes with 'delle cose belle', 'beautiful things'); they follow a kind of narrow trail which climbs—ours didn't rise whatsoever; it was horizontal; but theirs ascends to the stars. And perhaps that day, because of the presence of this water which seemingly ended up in a kind of swamp, I should have thought back on so many things that had struck me in the preceding years, deeply so, and that were, basically, always related to sacredness.

Notably the especially intense emotion that I had while discovering the Temple of Segesta, in Sicily, where we had gone with our friends from Vevey. A temple, as I later learnt, that had never been finished—I thought that it was a temple in ruins; there were columns that were very thick, strong, powerful, and very beautiful, but unfinished—and I should have thought of what that emotion had meant to me, that each temple I had been able to see on my trips, in Greece or elsewhere, were like cages that protected, contained and dissimulated sacredness.

On many other trips, the same kind of emotion was produced. It was always related to an insignificant religious site, to a small, even modest, even ordinary chapel, not even decorated, or to a crypt, and in fact I told myself that if I hadn't been rather obsessed with a kind of anti-clericalism that was ours at a given moment, in particular among my left-wing friends in Lausanne, I would have perhaps realized that in such places was something much more important than I could have initially imagined: truly this encounter—often unexpected, unhoped for, and yet . . . perhaps pursued by seeking it out—with the sacred.

While walking along an orchard—an almond orchard, or elsewhere a quince orchard—while entering, or passing by, I would again feel the same emotion. That of an open construction which seemingly contained the infinite. And each time with the truly central sentiment of sacredness.

So in fact I should have again taken up Hölderlin, who had surely been the most important encounter in my life as a poetry reader. The encounter had effaced or, rather, weakened my young man's natural admiration for Rilke. Hölderlin finally appeared to me to be superior, as a man, to Rilke, because he possessed a kind of absolutely insane purity, whereas Rilke was, all the same, a clever man who knew how to use his charm to seduce ladies into subsequently going out and buying him some L'origan perfume . . . Indeed, I should have returned to Hölderlin and, notably, to the opening of 'Patmos', perhaps the most beautiful hymn that he finished, before his mind went somewhat astray:

Nah ist
Und schwer zu fassen der Gott

[Near
And difficult to grasp is the god]

And especially the lines that follow:

Wo aber Gefahr ist, wächst
Das Rettende auch

[Yet where there's danger
also grows what can save]

He then speaks of eagles which nest in very steep places, very remote from each other, and addresses a kind of prayer to this god whom he had first said was ungraspable:

So gib unschuldig Wasser,
O Fittige gib uns . . .

[Give us innocent water,
Oh give us wings . . .]

Here in an extraordinary way, brought together in so few words, are the two privileged messages of poetry: birds and 'eau vive', 'live water', white water. And again I find the theme of the traveller who leaves and comes back. As if Hölderlin were expressing almost everything that is essential for me, in this beginning part of the poem, in a few lines of verse.

Time having passed, and rediscovering this beginning part of the poem that I had known very well for such a long time, I set out once again with a fresh start, as it were, in the direction of something that was undeniably La Clarté Notre-Dame.

Now, so late in my life, how this was becoming clear and profound!

Recalling these lines of verse, with everything that the mere name of 'Patmos' arouses in me, including the memory of Saint John who would have received I no longer know what illumination there, and thinking of those very steep mountains separated by an abyss, I would almost feel tempted to ask in turn for both 'innocent water' and wings for an unthinkable crossing, and yet . . .

The Last Book of the Madrigals

I

En écoutant Claudio Monteverdi

On croirait, quand il chante, qu'il appelle une ombre
qu'il aurait entrevue un jour dans la forêt
et qu'il faudrait, fût-ce au prix de son âme, retenir :
c'est par urgence que sa voix prend feu.

Alors, à sa lumière d'incendie, on aperçoit
un pré nocturne, humide, et la forêt par-delà
où il avait surpris cette ombre tendre,
ou beaucoup mieux et plus tendre qu'une ombre :

il n'y a plus que chênes et violettes, maintenant.

La voix qui a illuminé la distance retombe.

Je ne sais pas s'il a franchi le pré.

While Listening to Claudio Monteverdi

When singing, he seems to call to a shade
whom he glimpsed one day in the woods
and needs to hold on to, be his soul at stake:
the urgency makes his voice catch fire.

Then by its own blazing light, we spot a moist
night-time meadow and the woods beyond
where he had come across that tender shade
or much better and more tender than a shade:

now there's nothing but oaks and violets.

The voice that has brightened the distance fades.

I don't know if he has crossed the meadow.

Voici ce que j'ai cru l'entendre murmurer,
ce printemps-là, sur sa lyre brûlante et lasse :

« Je ne veux pas être conduit par vos trop candides anges
mais plutôt, même décevantes, par les douces,
les rieuses soudain qui sait pourquoi si sérieuses,
et nous prendrons pour lampe les cerisiers blancs. »

Pauvre fou ! Seraient-elles plus belles même
que la perle lunaire ou la boucle des Pléiades,
ou seraient-ils, les anges, plus tranquilles que les aigles,
ni ces sœurs de la terre, sa parure,
ni ces princes rapaces des hauteurs
ne lui feront franchir le pas sans grimacer.

À moins que justement, peut-être, justement,
dans ce débordement de la lumière,
en égarant, à leur manière elles ne guident,
parce qu'elles seraient les images les plus fidèles
de l'éphémère ciel ?

C'est leur regard que je regarde, assez longtemps
pour vérifier ces repères de mes pas futurs.

Here's what I thought I heard him murmur,
that spring, on his weary ardent lyre:

'I've no wish to be led away by your too-ingenuous angels,
but rather by those gentle women, even if they disappoint,
those merry ones suddenly—who knows why—so serious,
and we'll take the white cherry trees for a lamp.'

Poor fool! Be they more splendid even
than the lunar pearl or the buckle of the Pleiades,
or be the others, the angels, quieter than the eagles,
neither those sisters of the earth, its finery,
nor those princely raptors of the heights
will help him take the step without wincing.

Unless just for that reason, perhaps, just for that,
in this overflowing light—
would their way of leading astray also guide,
since they'd be the most faithful images
of the ephemeral sky?

It's their gaze I gaze at, for quite a while,
to verify these landmarks for my future steps.

La fête allait finir. Je me suis arrêté,
j'ai écouté sans dire mot.
Quelques-uns devisaient encore, à voix très basse,
de l'équipée lointaine d'Alexandre. D'autres
se regardaient entre les franges de leurs cils :
jamais ils n'auront bu de vin plus ivre qu'en ces coupes.

Puis j'ai levé les yeux : toute la largeur du ciel
était autour de nous
avec un grésillement dans les éteules
comme d'étoiles à ras de terre.
Un dernier vol, telle une trace de silence, fut visible
et je me dis : « Nous voilà donc nés de nouveau
par le baptême de la longue nuit d'été. »

The feast was going to end. I stopped,
listening without saying a word.
Some were still conversing, in low voices,
about Alexander's distant venture, others
peering at each other through their eyelashes:
never will they have drunk a headier wine than from those cups.

Then I raised my eyes: the whole wide sky
was around us,
with chirping in the stubble
like stars along the ground.
A last flight, like a trail of silence, was visible
and I said to myself: 'So now we're born again,
baptized by the long summer night.'

Le chariot

Comme dans les Triomphes peints aux murs d'heureux palais,
mais, celui-ci, ni de la Mort ni de l'Amour,
de la Grâce plutôt, je pense, ou du Plaisir,
à travers les collines colorées par l'été,
comme il montait plus haut que les derniers arbres,
j'ai cru qu'avec le grincement de ses planches et de ses roues,
il allait, ce chariot, pour un peu, dès que le jour
aurait éteint ses feux, rejoindre l'autre,
où chacun n'aurait plus qu'à tendre à peine la main
pour se gorger d'étoiles mûres.

The Chariot

As in those Triumphs painted on happy palace walls,
yet this one neither of Death, nor of Love,
but rather, I think, of Grace, or of Pleasure,
across the summer-tinged hills,
then as it rose above the last trees,
I believed that with its creaking wood and wheels,
once the day had snuffed out its fires, this chariot
would almost join the other one
where each of us would hardly have to reach
to gorge ourselves on ripe stars.

Le vin avait coulé en abondance dans les verres,
tel un sang plus léger qui ne naîtrait pas des blessures.
« À la beauté du monde ! » fut-il dit, et « À telle beauté
parmi nous, grave ou rieuse ! » « À la douleur du monde ! »
eût-on pu entendre en écho, si tout ce vin
était redevenu du sang dans nos verres ébréchés.

The wine had kept flowing into the glasses
like a lighter blood born of no wounds.
'To the beauty of the world!' it was said, and 'To this beauty
among us, be she solemn or merry!' 'To the world's pain!'
could have been heard in echo if all this wine
had turned back into blood in our chipped glasses.

Beaucoup plus tard, j'ai vu
le vieux forgeron de volutes et de flammes
déposer ses outils :

toute sa gloire courtoise,
sa patiente science
en un instant devenues vaines
pour cette braise qui a sauté contre son cœur.

Much later I saw
the old blacksmith of volutes and flames
put down his tools:

all his courtly glory,
his patient skill
in an instant become vain
for this ember that had leapt to his heart.

Délirait-il quand je l'entendis murmurer :

« Si cette lampe qui est pareille à une ruche
est éloignée de moi,
si ce parfum s'éloigne, compagnons,
vous pouvez emporter ces liasses blanches et ces plumes :
où l'on m'emmène je n'en aurai plus l'usage . . . »

Was he delirious when I heard him murmur:

'If this lamp that is like a beehive
is removed from me,
if this perfume drifts away, companions,
you can carry off these quills and bundles of paper:
where I'm being led, I'll have no more use for them . . .'

Au printemps de cette année-là, comme j'avais l'esprit imprégné de musiques, de paroles, d'images italiennes qui s'étaient déposées en moi depuis mon premier voyage là-bas, à vingt et un ans, apercevant trois dames dans un jardin de buis, à contre-jour, auréolées par le timide soleil d'avril et portant toutes trois de légères robes blanches, je m'étais rappelé l'un des rares poèmes heureux de Dante :

> *Guido, i'vorrei che tu e Lapo ed io*
> *fossimo presi per incantamento*

où, s'adressant à son ami Cavalcanti, il rêve qu'un enchanteur, comme dans la légende arthurienne, leur procure un « vaisseau » pour les emmener à leur gré, eux deux et un autre ami poète ; et surtout, que soient présentes à bord leurs compagnes : « monna Vanna », « monna Lagia » et, pour lui-même, Dante, une dame qu'il dissimule derrière le nombre trente :

> *e ciascuna di lor fosse contenta*
> *si come i'credo que saremmo noi*

(« et nulle d'elles qui n'en fût contente / comme je crois que nous serions aussi »).

In the spring of that year, I had recalled one of Dante's rare cheerful poems after spotting against the sunlight and haloed by the timid April sun—with my mind full of the Italian music, words and images that had settled in me ever since my first trip to the country at the age of twenty-one—three ladies in a boxwood garden, all wearing light, white dresses:

Guido, i'vorrei che tu e Lapo ed io
fossimo presi per incantamento

Addressing his friend Cavalcanti, he dreams that an enchanter, as in the Arthurian legend, procures a 'vessel' for them so that they and another poet-friend can go wherever they wish; and especially that their female companions would also be aboard: 'Monna Vanna', 'Monna Lagia' and for himself, Dante, a lady that he dissimulates behind the number 'thirty', adding:

e ciascuna di lor fosse contenta
si come i'credo que saremmo noi

('and each of them would be content / as, I believe, we also would be')

Me remémorant ce poème si tendre, si heureux, si clair, j'aurais voulu — cela peut sembler de la dernière prétention, mais je ne pensais même pas à cet aspect des choses, qui n'avait aucune importance — en intégrer quelques vers dans un poème d'aujourd'hui qui en aurait poursuivi autrement la rêverie, telle qu'elle avait commencé à m'entraîner à mon tour. Je n'y suis pas parvenu. Ce que j'aurais voulu dire, c'est que, à peine, ayant vu ces trois « dames » et les entendant rire, m'étais-je imaginé que je pourrais monter avec elles dans quelque barque, j'avais vu mes mains déjà tachées par l'âge ; de sorte que le poème, parlant de moi à la troisième personne comme pour signifier une distance et le refus de toute illusion, se serait poursuivi peut-être ainsi :

Alors, désenvoûté, peut-être les priera-t-il
de monter avec lui plutôt dans l'autre barque
— si on le leur concède — afin de détourner de lui
l'assaut des brumes de plus en plus froides
qui l'attendent. Mais je sais
qu'à leur grâce il n'imposera pas telle équipée...

Qu'il se contente d'être au milieu d'elles rien
    de plus
qu'une ombre tendre, attentive, à peine triste,
que nulle, dans leur troupe heureuse, n'aura
    même vue.

Recalling the poem, which is so tender, so cheerful, so clear, I wanted to incorporate—this can seem pretentious, but I wasn't even thinking of this aspect of things, which had no importance—a few lines of it into a contemporary poem that would have prolonged the reverie differently, such as it had in turn begun to lead me. I didn't succeed in doing so. Having seen those three 'ladies' and listened to them laughing, I would have wanted to say, just as soon as I had imagined that I could climb into some skiff with them, I had seen my hands already spotted with age; so that the poem, speaking of me in the third person as if to signify a distance and the refusal of any illusion, would perhaps have continued thus:

> Thus, freed from the spell, perhaps he'll invite them
> to climb with him into the other skiff instead
> —if this be granted to them—to ward off
> the assault of the ever-colder haze
> awaiting him. But I know he won't impose
> such a jaunt upon their gracefulness ...
>
> May he content himself with being in their midst, nothing more
> than a shade—tender, attentive, hardly sad,
> whom no one in their happy crew will even have seen.

(Et je pense aujourd'hui que, pour cette autre barque, devait m'être revenu à l'esprit encore un autre poème italien, moderne celui-là et que j'avais eu à traduire, non sans peine, tant il est tourmenté, quelques années auparavant : le dernier poème d'Ungaretti, écrit à plus de quatre-vingts ans, où il voit de « sinistres barques » dériver dans les parages rocailleux de la mort.)

(And today I think that another Italian poem must have come to mind a few years earlier with respect to that other skiff—a modern poem, which I had translated not without difficulty, anguished as it is. It was written when Ungaretti was more than eighty years old, and it is his last poem, in which he sees 'sinister skiffs' drifting in the rocky waters of death.)

II

Les ruisseaux se sont réveillés.

La voix moins claire s'entrelace à la plus claire
comme se tressent leurs rapides eaux.

Pour qu'on me lie avec des liens pareils,
je veux bien tendre les deux mains.

Ainsi lié, je me délivre de l'hiver.

The streams have awakened.

The least clear voice intertwines with the clearest one
as their fast waters weave together.

So that I can be bound with similar bonds,
I'm happy to reach out my two hands.

Thus bound, I free myself from winter.

Le tissu bleu du ciel,
Pénélope à chaque aube, charitable, le retisse
(ou s'y emploie la nuit avec ses peignes cloutés d'or),

moins pour décourager ses frivoles prétendants
que pour, patiente et fidèle, nous protéger
de l'archer noir aux trop froides flèches.

At every dawn charitable Penelope
reweaves the blue cloth of the sky
(or applies herself to it at night with her gold-studded combs)

less to discourage frivolous suitors
than to protect us patiently and faithfully
from the black archer with his too-frigid arrows.

Vert, rose et bleu
dans l'éclat violent du jour.

Élisez donc ces couleurs, jockeys prompts de l'été,
portez-les à la gloire de l'invisible parieuse
qui a misé sur votre fougue sa beauté,

vert cru, rose angélique et bleu d'iris . . .

Green, pink and blue
in the violent daytime glare.

Choose these colours, swift jockeys of summer,
wear them to glorify the invisible woman
who bet her beauty on your fiery spirit,

raw green, angelic pink and iris blue . . .

Vert, rose et bleu,

nouez-vous en écharpe à l'épaule du champion solaire
debout, lance au poing, dans l'arène des moissons.

Celle qu'il sert, pour peu qu'elle baisse les yeux,
lui fera culbuter le vieux squelette ennemi
sous sa cuirasse noire.

Qui, autour de l'arène, sur ces bancs en feu, douterait
que la grâce vivante ne triomphe d'un fagot d'os ?

Et, pour trophée, au sourire ambigu
il offrira le funèbre ivoire éclaté sous son épieu.

Green, pink and blue,

scarf yourselves around the shoulder of the solar champion
standing, gripping his lance, in the arena of harvests.

She whom he serves, should she lower her eyes,
will knock over the old enemy skeleton
behind his black breastplate.

Who on those flaming benches around the arena would doubt
that living grace will triumph over a bundle of bones?

And for a trophy, with an ambiguous smile,
he'll offer the funereal ivory shattered by his spear.

Bleu, vert et rose,

et les figues pendent dans les feuilles comme de fortes cloches
pleines de semence de bélier.

Blue, green and pink,

and the figs hang in the leaves like sturdy bells
full of ram semen.

Regardez les martinets :
ils sont autant de traits de fer forgés dans les murs,
décochés vers les quatre angles du ciel
quand tombe le soir d'été.

Alors, je crois entendre le vieux musicien,
forgeron, lui, de volutes et de flammes,
pour la dernière fois peut-être supplier :

« Belle archère, détournez de moi votre arme,
que je ne pâlisse ni m'effondre comme ces nuées. »

Ou ne seraient-ils pas plutôt, ces oiseaux, des hameçons jetés
pour retenir par ses écailles juillet trop fuyant ?

Et lui d'écrire encore, sur les dernières portées,
peut-être, de sa vie :

« Telle inconnue pêchant dans sa barque légère
m'a ferré moi aussi.

Si j'ai cru doux d'abord d'être sa proie,
maintenant le fer tire sur mon cœur
et je ne sais si c'est le jour ou moi qui perd son sang
dans ces eaux nacrées. »

Look at the swifts:
as many wrought-iron arrows in the walls,
shot towards the four corners of the sky
when the summer evening falls.

Then I believe I'm hearing the old musician,
the blacksmith of volutes and flames,
perhaps imploring for the last time:

'Beautiful archeress, point your weapon away from me
so I won't pale and collapse like those clouds.'

Or wouldn't those birds instead be cast fishhooks
to catch too quickly fleeting July by its scales?

And he who still writes on the last staffs,
perhaps, of his life:

'That unknown woman fishing in her lightweight skiff
has struck me as well.

I first thought it sweet to be her prey,
but now the hook tugs at my heart
and I don't know if it's the daylight or me
bleeding in these pearly waters.'

Tous les blés flambent
et la brève alouette
est un fragment ascendant de ce feu.
Elle ne gravit tous les paliers de l'air
que parce que le sol est trop brûlant.

Il est une beauté que les yeux et les mains touchent
et qui fait faire au cœur un premier degré dans le chant.
Mais l'autre se dérobe et il faut s'élever plus haut
jusqu'à ce que nous autres ne voyions plus rien,
la belle cible et le chasseur tenace
confondus dans la jubilation de la lumière.

All the wheat is ablaze
and the brief skylark
a fragment rising from this fire.
It scales all the levels of the air
only because the ground is burning hot.

There's a beauty that the eyes and hands touch
and that makes the heart take a first step in song.
But the other one steals away and we must climb higher
until we can't see anything any more,
the beautiful target and the tenacious hunter
blended in the jubilant light.

Considérez le ciel solaire
à l'heure de l'extrême incandescence :
c'est là qu'il nous faut traverser.

Des barques croisent dans ce lac de lumière.

Aiguisez mieux votre regard :
vous les verrez franchir sans bruit cette brume éblouie
et, par-delà, s'ancrer dans les eaux de la nuit
pour y plonger éternellement leurs filets
                                    dans les profondeurs.

Ponder the solar sky
at its most incandescent:
this is what we must cross.

Skiffs fare forth in this lake of light.

Sharpen your gaze:
you'll see them silently drifting through this dazzled haze
and, further on, anchoring in the waters of the night
to sink their nets forever there

                                into the depths.

Qui la dirait comète ne parlerait pas en vain,
cette clarté, visible rarement en une vie
et dans la mienne, je le crains, pour la dernière fois.

Celle d'espaces inconnus venue
et chargée de tous les parfums de la distance,
la nomade à jamais des noirs déserts,
j'aurai dans ses légers cheveux rêvé de perdre le sommeil.

Calling her a comet wouldn't be speaking in vain—
this brightness, rarely seen in a lifetime
and in mine, I fear, for the last time.

A brightness come from unknown spaces
and fully fragrant with the distance,
the nomad woman forever of dark deserts—
I'll have dreamt of losing sleep in her wispy hair.

Abeilles, accourez broder de braise ces robes
ou ces paupières, ou ces lèvres, ou ce cou,

puis, moins brûlantes mais non moins dorées,
éparpillez-vous sur toute la soie de la nuit.

Bees, come flying to embroider embers into these dresses
or these eyelids, or these lips, or this neck,

then, burning less but no less golden,
scatter yourselves over all the silk of the night.

Pour quelques pas qu'il aurait faits près d'elle dans la nuit,
je pressens qu'il l'aurait placée,
comme on l'a fait pour Andromède ou Bételgeuse,
au plus haut de son ciel intérieur,
entre les cornes de la Lyre,
afin que jusque dans l'hiver glacial
il puisse encore voir étinceler
les traces des trop tendres griffes sur son cœur.

For a few steps he would have taken near her in the night
I sense that he would have placed her,
as had been done for Andromeda or Betelgeuse,
in the highest part of his inner sky,
between the horns of Lyra,
so that even in icy winter
he could still see the sparkling
too-tender talon marks on his heart.

Mais que va-t-il la comparer aux froides figures du ciel ?

Parle à sa place, corps, toi qui la comprends mieux :
murmure que c'est au contraire comme si
le Cygne insaisissable entrait enfin dans notre chambre
et qu'il nous eût frôlé de son regard ou de ses plumes . . .

But what's he doing comparing her to cold celestial figures?

Speak for him, body, you who understand her better:
murmur that it is, on the contrary, as if
the ungraspable Swan at last entered our bedroom
and brushed up against us with his gaze or his feathers . . .

La lumière n'est plus aujourd'hui qu'un lit de plumes pour le repos du cœur.

Ah! plutôt, qu'elle vienne, celle qui, même endormie, la froisserait de sa rosée comme une rose!

Today the light is but a bed of feathers
to rest the heart.

Ah! may she come instead, she who, even asleep,
will rumple that light with her dew like a rose!

Écarte cette lumière qui n'a jamais d'yeux
comme un rideau inutile et entre,
approche, toi qui regardes et qui parles,
plus touchante que l'air d'automne,
plus tendre que toute sa laine et tout son lait.

Push away this light that never has eyes,
like a useless curtain, and come in,
come closer, you who can look and speak,
and are more touching than autumn air,
more tender than all its wool and all its milk.

Là-bas, les tentes bleues des montagnes
semblent vides.

Qu'ourdissez-vous de sombre sur vos fils,
oiseaux nerveux, mes familières hirondelles ?

Qu'allez-vous, à vous toutes, m'enlever ?

Si ce n'était que la lumière de l'été,
j'attendrais bien ici votre retour.

Si ce n'était que ma vie, emportez-la.

Mais la lumière de ma vie, oiseaux cruels,
laissez-la-moi pour éclairer novembre.

In the distance, the blue tents of the mountains
seem empty.

What are you sombrely scheming on your wires,
nervous birds, my familiar swallows?

What are you all going to take away from me?

If it were only the summer light
I'd willingly wait here for your return.

If it were only my life, carry it off.

But the light of my life, cruel birds,
let me keep it so I can brighten November.

Automne imminent,
je frissonne sous ton manteau de plumes de coq :

décidément, je te ressemble trop,
héraut bariolé du froid !

Encore si je n'avais pas à porter sur les épaules
ces deux tristesses désunies
et toutes les autres
comme une charge de neige à venir !

Largement de quoi se voûter à tout jamais.

Imminent autumn,
I shiver under your rooster-feather coat:

I obviously look too much like you,
many-colored herald of the cold!

If only I didn't have to shoulder
these two disunited sadnesses
and all the others
like a load of forthcoming snow!

It's more than enough to make me stoop for ever.

Bûcheron de genévriers,
ce que tu portes au bûcher sur tes épaules,
seraient-ce de vieux bois de cerf ?

D'ailleurs : es-tu le bûcheron, toi-même,
ou le cerf ?

Bûcheron, que ta hache se retourne contre toi :
cerf harassé,
implore Diane de t'achever vite
avant que la forêt ne saigne de tous ses arbres !

Lumberjack of junipers,
would what you're shouldering to the woodshed
be old deer antlers?

Moreover: are you yourself the lumberjack
or the deer?

Lumberjack, may your axe turn against you:
worn-out deer,
implore Diana to kill you off fast
before all the trees in the forest bleed!

Et maintenant, tu te retrouves seul devant le feu
dans ta cabane.

Les flammes semblent étouffer le bois comme du lierre.

N'y a-t-il vraiment plus ici d'autre ombre que toi ?

As-tu rêvé que la lumière n'était pas seulement au ciel,
hors de portée,
pas seulement dans la musique entendue
mais dans la musicienne, sur ses lèvres,
dans ses yeux, même quand elle se tait ?

Ne dis pas que tu as rêvé, ne le crois pas :
simplement, tu n'étais pas digne.

Bûcheron gourd ou loup naïf, ne sors donc plus
de tes forêts : la neige y compte sur toi.

Heureusement, la hache est posée loin de tes mains.

And now, you find yourself alone in front of the fire
in your cabin.

The flames seem to smother the wood like ivy.

Is there really no other shade here any more but you?

Have you dreamt that the light was not only in the sky,
out of reach,
not only in the music heard,
but in the musician, on her lips,
in her eyes even when she grows silent?

Don't say you've been dreaming, don't believe it:
simply, you were unworthy.

Numb lumberjack or naive wolf, don't leave
your forests any more: the snow counts on you there.

Luckily, the axe has been placed far from your hands.

Afterword

'Leaning Back Against the Night'[*]

'And yet . . .' With these words comes to an end—or not
to an end—*La Clarté Notre-Dame*, the last book written
by Philippe Jaccottet, who passed away on 24 February
2021. The two words moderate the assertion, veer and
turn thought in another direction . . . Like a hesitant
river, the text goes on its way, henceforth out of sight,
in remote lands. This sudden reservation, this impossi-
bility to give in completely to a too-simple certitude, are
at the heart of the poet's work.

---

[*] Originally titled 'Adossé à la nuit', this article first appeared in
Po&sie (Autumn 2021).

The word 'yet'—'sarinagara' in Japanese—concludes a poem that Kobayashi Issa wrote upon the death of his child—five syllables that the French novelist Philippe Forest uses for the title of one of his books. He too is mourning his little daughter's death. Telling and half-imagining the life of Issa, the great haiku master, Forest questions the unthinkable: How can one survive when facing the unacceptable death of a child, when facing war and destruction, and an ordeal caused by the most heart-rending kind of truth? How can one remain standing? To whom can one confide, from the depths of one's despair, 'the care of one's life', if not to the memory of a desire?—for 'there is something, in a human being's heart, that cannot resign itself completely [. . .] something still persists when everything is over'.[1]

Jaccottet selected Issa's poem for his anthology, *Haïku*, published by Éditions Fata Morgana in 1996. Here are a few lines from the French translation:

Ce monde, une rosée,
Je le veux bien:
Pourtant, pourtant . . .

[This world, mere dew,
I do want it:
Yet, yet . . .]

---

1 Philippe Forest, *Sarinagara* (Paris: Gallimard-Folio, 2004), pp. 93–4.

Life is but a passage, indeed . . . but at the moment of consenting to this obvious fact, as if echoing the poem that Issa wrote in a painful feeling of helplessness, Jaccottet takes a step to the side and, with a last-minute rectification, reopens the debate. For 'something still persists when everything is over'.

*

Jaccottet's entire *oeuvre* leans back against the night, the night of human beings, the night of the world. Sometimes he resorts to formulations of a rare violence:

'I must contain in one invisible reality
Both source and ashes, lips and a dead rat's
    carcass'[2]

'A human . . . hazard of the air
[. . .]
then rip the breath away: and he rots'[3]

His treatise on love and despair, *The Last Book of Madrigals*, concludes with the terrifying words that the poet addresses himself in a benumbing image:

---

2 Philippe Jaccottet, *Oeuvres complètes* (Paris: Gallimard-Pléiade, 2014), p. 353. [In English: *Seedtime* (Tess Lewis trans.) (London: Seagull, 2003), p. 36.]

3 Jaccottet, 'Leçons' in *Oeuvres*, p. 458. [In English: *Leçons/ Learning* (Mark Treharne trans.) (Birmingham, UK: Delos Press, 2001), p. 38.]

'Luckily, the axe has been placed far from your hands'

In *La Clarté Notre-Dame*, the ignominy, still harsher and more direct, 'soils' the light and turns it 'into a lure that would make you vomit'.

Without overemphasizing the blackness of despair, nor employing excessive metaphors, but instead mustering a force that never failed him, including his last writings, Jaccottet always attempted to ward off his demons. One recalls the cockcrows that are likened to cries for help and are heart-rending in their distress, or those lamentations, so frequent in his notebooks, that haunt his nightmares. Or the sinister bell in *Chants d'en bas* [Songs from Below], that is, the bell of old age that goes out of kilter in a 'belfry of bones'[4] . . . 'And yet' he keeps coming back to the beauty of one of Baudelaire's lines, to his own emotion in front of an almond or quince orchard; or he endeavours to describe the sweetness of gillyflowers or the heady fragrance of iris . . . This chiaroscuro runs through his *oeuvre*. His unique salvation: a few traces of a fleeting intensity and the music of favourite readings, which he tenderly gathers around him in *La Clarté Notre-Dame*, as if to cover himself with a comforter of feathers, before lying down in the skiff and releasing the rope

---

4 From the 'Autres chants' [Other Songs] section of *Chants d'en bas* [Songs from Below]. See *Oeuvres*, p. 549.

. . . Moses heading back out on the Nile for a last voyage no longer at the onset—but in the evening of his life.

Given a discreet chronological rhythm, the themes of *La Clarté Notre-Dame*—recurring as the prose progresses over a period of several years like a lied sung from beginning to end by the same voice—seek to maintain this balancing act: What can keep the worst in equilibrium? How can one come out of despair? Facing 'fright at losing space',[5] there is song . . . With striking clarity, a clarity sometimes crepuscular but never muddled or approximate, the prose spirals slowly forward, the author retracing his steps, opening and closing parentheses, with brief halts and moments in which he recovers control, everything uniting in an ultimate vision of appeasement and fragility.

Like an obsessive litany which wavers between two unreconcilable realities—the screams of humans tortured in a Damascus prison and a tiny monastery bell—the book comes back to the age-old questions: Where are the gods? Is it worthwhile? Why reiterate what has been said . . . ? What's the purpose? . . . These questions are raised in *Through an Orchard*; *Landscapes with Absent Figures*; *A Notebook of Greenery*, and many other books by the author-poet. But now the questions have become

---

5 From 'Airs' in *Oeuvres*, p. 421.

graver, unburdened of all rhetoric: this new and final volume is a long recitative which is sung over the abysses like a *basso continuo*, a 'lesson of darkness' which is pronounced over the ruins of Aleppo, and which attempts, in passing, to retain *in extremis* a few pure moments of marvelling . . . like a voyager who is on the brink of emptiness and reaches out his hand one last time towards his travelling companions: Leopardi, Dante, Claudel; Sophocles' *Antigone*, Cristina Campo, Shestov, Goethe; or Du Bouchet, Rilke, Hölderlin . . . like so many stars above an arid path.

In a Proustian manner, the prose moves forward in successive echoes, with the madeleine cookie being the faint yet limpid sound of a bell in the evening light, the bell of La Clarté Notre-Dame monastery, a sound which ventures forth with an almost bold bravery over the hills, reminding the poet, from his childhood, of the tiny snow-covered bell on the garden gate of his uncle's house where he would go with his family, every winter, to celebrate New Year's Day. A real bell awakening the shrill tinkling of a ghostly bell, and in the process his entire memory becomes an old man's horizon. In this testament, Jaccottet, who has reached the far end of his life, traces an arch between old age and childhood, and in a handful of pages brings together the horror of violence, his fright at death, the anguish of the final appointment, and a boundless gratitude for existence. Because 'not all the attention must be given to misfortune'.[6]

*

When Jaccottet asked me to compile the manuscript of *La Clarté Notre-Dame* from his notes and preliminary texts, his request had filled me with great melancholy. I knew that it would be our last 'meeting'. Twice, in May and then in June 2020, I drove down from Lausanne to Grignan to speak with him, each time for a little more than a week. Our conversations were mostly about old memories, but Jaccottet would also, in successive waves, return to his fears, his preoccupations, and his readings. He was true to himself. As we sat next to each other at the window, we would begin by speaking of unimportant matters, as if to divert from what he was himself going over in his mind. He seemed to be a very old bonze with a diaphanous face, a tissue-paper face, friable and almost transparent, a fragile incarnation of a human being, so fragile that one could fear, when breathing, to blow out a flame so frail . . . I would venture a few words, almost ill at ease to be there with my moods, my colourful clothing, my bags, my bracelets, and my mobile phone

---

6 Philippe Jaccottet, *Taches de soleil, ou d'ombre* (Gouville-sur-Mer, France: Le Bruit du temps, 2013), p. 180. [In English: *Patches of Sunlight, or of Shadow* (John Taylor trans.) (London: Seagull, 2021), p. 226.]

... Sometimes a great silence would settle in between us. Almost speechless, his eyes half-shut, he seemed to be moving way from the living ...

And yet ... because of a word, an association of ideas, a detail grasped in mid-flight, his eyes would suddenly reopen, seek out the window, and his face, beaming and youthful, would come back to life; with a firmer voice, he would take delight in an anecdote or a trivial everyday event, picking up wherever he had left off with a sure sense of authority and an infallible memory. A double standard ... At once destitute and upright.

A poet of nuance and attenuation, Jaccottet has always wavered between opposite poles, preferring a middle way to extremes. But nuance demands time ... and often seems to be a non-choice. It is a risk that one must run. Jaccottet accepts this risk with each new book, moderating his intuitions, seeking the exact measurement of each thing, even if it means cracking the cohesion of univocal thinking. Deeply preoccupied by the rise of evil in today's world, he experienced moments of great desperation, to the extent of feeling that all literature was stricken with powerlessness. However, he espoused no ideology or political cause. Nothing could appease his torment when he faced what is absurd or incomprehensible. Fleeing from lures and certitudes, at a far remove from simple convictions, he questions himself, in book after book, and seeks an equilibrium: 'There is perhaps a connection, and not only a contradiction, between hell and flowers'.[7]

Ranging from brightness to darkness, and from darkness to brightness, he has never given up this journey, all the while temporarily finding a meaning, a kind of appeasement: 'This in-between space, this open enclosure—perhaps my only homeland.'[8] When everything closes back up and becomes blurred, when a high wall rises in front of him, the emotion returns; and by means of the sudden protesting burst 'and yet . . .', a true breath of air, the poet reappropriates the doubt—and with it, the dream—in the darkness that surrounds him. His greatest force is his perpetually renewed desire, during the most terrifying night, to head for the light.

What more precious thing could he hand down to us than this eternal discomfort? And what better transaction with existence than not finishing what he was saying? Jaccottet possesses the art of the *post scriptum*, opening his books with a recommencement in which the movement of his thinking persists well beyond the words,

---

7 From 'Cahier de verdure' [Notebook of Greenery] in *Oeuvres*, p. 775. [In English: *And, Nonetheless: Selected Prose and Poetry 1990–2009* (John Taylor trans.) (New York: Chelsea Editions, 2011), p. 119.]
8 From 'Et, néanmoins' [And, Nonetheless] in *Oeuvres*, p. 1108. [In English: *And, Nonetheless*, p. 237.]

'for there is no reason, for a novelist, that everything ends with life'.[9] As luminously serious sustenance, *La Clarté Notre-Dame*, forever incomplete, hands over to the reader the care of pursuing . . .

June 2021

---

9 Forest, *Sarinagara*, p. 207.

Unless otherwise noted, all translations are mine.

La Clarté Notre-Dame

PAGE 7 | Jaccottet's *Requiem* was reissued in 1991 by Éditions Fata Morgana. The passage that he quotes here is from *suivi de Remarques* (Paris: Fata Morgana, 1990, pp. 46–47) included as an afterword to his long poem. See Philippe Jaccottet, *Oeuvres complètes* (Paris: Gallimard-Pléiade, 2014), pp. 1279–94.

PAGE 8 | 'so few noises' alludes to Jaccottet's book of poems *Ce peu de bruits* (2008; in *Oeuvres*, pp. 1215–70). For the English translation, see 'These Slight Noises' in *And, Nonetheless: Selected Prose and Poetry 1990–2007* (John Taylor trans.) (New York: Chelsea Editions, 2011).

Pierre Jean Jouve's *Dans les années profondes* (In the Deep Years) is included in his *Oeuvre*, VOL. II (Jean Starobinski ed.) (Paris: Mercure de France, 1987), pp. 959–1050.

PAGE 12 | For Jaccottet's reference to Saint-Blaise, see *Paysages avec figures absentes* (1976; in *Oeuvres*, pp. 510–12), especially p. 511, where he mentions an egret suddenly flying up. For the English translation, see *Landscapes with Absent Figures* (Mark Treharne trans.) (Birmingham, UK: Delos Press, 1997).

PAGE 18 | Apropos of Syria, Jaccottet refers to his book *Un calme feu* (2007). For the English translation, see *A Calm Fire and Other Travel Writings* (John Taylor trans.) (London: Seagull Books, 2019).

PAGE 19 | 'unequal combat'—alludes to Jaccottet's book of poems *Le Combat inégal* (Chêne-Bourg, Switzerland: La Dogana, 2010). See also Jaccottet's acceptance speech for the Grand Prix Schiller, 'Le Combat inégal' in *Oeuvres*, pp. 1342–46.

'building himself a rampart'—Jaccottet recalls René Char's wish to build a rampart out of twigs which in turn refers to the latter's prose text entitled 'Le Rempart de brindilles'. See René Char, *Oeuvres complètes* (Paris: Gallimard-Pléaide, 1983), pp. 359–62.

PAGE 23 | 'Livre des morts' (Book of the Dead) is the final section of Jaccottet's poetry volume *L'Ignorant* (1958; in *Oeuvres*, pp. 170–74). *Leçons* (1969; in *Oeuvres*, pp. 449–60) is a long poetic sequence that evokes the death of Jaccottet's father-in-law, Louis Haesler. For the English translation, see *Leçons / Learning . . .* (Mark Treharne trans.) (Birmingham, UK: Delos Press, 2001).

'Exsultate, jubilate' (Exult, rejoice), K. 165, refers to the 1773 motet by Mozart.

PAGE 24 | 'As if from the splendid . . . on high'—from Hölderlin's poem, 'Am Quell der Donau', which begins with: 'Denn, wie wenn hoch von der herrlichgestimmten, der Orgel / Im heiligen Saal'. See Friedrich Hölderlin,

Sämtliche Gedichte (Berlin: Deutscher Klassiker, 1992),
p. 321.

PAGE 25 | '*almond-tree flowers*'—alludes to the Palestinian
poet Mahmoud Darwish's poem 'To Describe an Almond
Blossom'; see *Almond Blossoms and Beyond* (Mohammad
Shaheen trans.) (Northampton, MA: Interlink Publishing,
2009), p. 20:

> If a writer were to compose a successful piece
> describing the almond blossom, the fog would rise
> from the hills, and people, all the people, would say:
> This is it.
> These are the words of our national anthem.

PAGE 27 | In regard to the 'Very High', Plotinus held the
doctrine that the soul possessed a 'higher part' that was
essentially a being in the divine, intelligible realm.

'those signs of which Hölderlin . . . "help heaven"'—Jaccottet
refers to the following stanza in Hölderlin's poem 'Die
Titanen' (*Sämtliche Gedichte*, p. 391):

> Mich aber umsummet
> Die Bien und wo der Ackersmann
> Die Furchen machet singen gegen
> Dem Lichte die Vögel. Manche helfen
> Dem Himmel. Diese sieht
> Der Dichter . . .

> [But around me buzzes
> The bee and where the ploughman
> Makes his furrows the birds
> Sing towards the light. Many things
> Help heaven. This the poet
> Sees . . .]

PAGE 31 | 'Liturgy . . . necessary than useful'—Campo's words,
'Liturgia—come poesia—è splendore gratuito, spreco

delicato, più necessario dell'utile', from the poem 'Note sopra la liturgia'. See Cristina Campo, *Sotto falso nome* (Milan: Adelphi, 1998), pp. 127–9.

'A riddle, what springs up purely'—Hölderlin's line, 'Ein Rätsel ist Reinentsprungenes', from the fourth strophe of the poem 'Der Rhein'; see *Sämtliche Gedichte*, p. 329.

Paul Claudel's play, *Tête d'Or*, was first staged in 1889, with a definitive version in 1894.

PAGE 32 | 'Les voyageurs . . . voix endormies'—A haiku by the Japanese poet Taigi Sumi (1709–71) as translated into French by Jaccottet; see *Haïku* (Paris: Fata Morgana, 2010), n.p.

PAGE 33 | One of Goethe's famous poems, 'Wandrers Nachtlied', has often been translated into English, including by Henry Wordsworth Longfellow as 'Wanderer's Nightsong' (1845):

> Über allen Gipfeln
> Ist Ruh,
> In allen Wipfeln
> Spürest du
> Kaum einen Hauch;
> Die Vögelein schweigen im Walde.
> Warte nur, balde
> Ruhest du auch.

> ['O'er all the hill-tops
> Is quiet now,
> In all the tree-tops
> Hearest thou
> Hardly a breath;
> The birds are asleep in the trees:
> Wait; soon like these
> Thou too shalt rest.]

'In queste sale antiche'—the lines from Giacomo Leopardi's poem 'Ricordanze' are found in the third strophe:

> In queste sale antiche,
> Al chiaror delle nevi, intorno a queste
> Ampie finestre sibilando il vento,
> Rimbombaro i sollazzi e le festose
> Mie voce al tempo che l'acerbo, indegno
> Mistero delle cose a noi si mostra
> Pien di dolcezza . . .

Here is Jonathan Galassi's translation—see Giacomo Leopardi's *Canti* (New York: Farrar Straus Giroux, 2010, p. 183)—which offers a different interpretation of the first two lines:

> In these ancient rooms
> reflecting the snow's brightness, with the wind
> whistling in these wide windows,
> the sound of games and my glad shouting
> echoed in the moment when the cruel,
> unworthy mystery of things appears to us
> as full of sweetness

In the same strophe, Leopardi writes: 'queste dipinte mura, / Quei figurati armenti' ('these painted walls / those pictured herds').

Jaccottet's remark about the 'silvery sonority' of Leopardi's verse is from a note, dated November 1980, in *La Seconde Semaison* (Paris: Gallimard, 1996, p. 22; in *Oeuvres*, p. 868). For the English translation, see *The Second Seedtime* (Tess Lewis trans.) (London: Seagull Books, 2017), p. 13.

PAGE **34** | 'leading me back to . . . du Bouchet'—Jaccottet pays tribute to his friend, the poet André du Bouchet (1924–2001), and discusses Hölderlin's poem in *Truinas*. For the English translation, see *Truinas, 21 April 2001* (John Taylor trans.) (Les Brouzils, France: Fortnightly Review, 2018), pp. 18–19.

Hölderlin's lines are from the fragment 'Entwurf zu Kolomb IV'. See Martin Heidegger, *Erläuterungen zu Hölderlins Dichtung* (Frankfurt: Vittorio Klostermann, 1951), p.395:

> Von wegen geringer Dinge
> Verstimmt wie vom Schnee war
> Die Glocke, womit
> Man laütet
> Zum Abendessen.

Du Bouchet alludes to the same fragment in the title of his volume *Désaccordée comme par de la neige* (1989).

PAGE **40** | 'the admirable ending . . . *Inferno*'—The last lines of Dante's *Inferno* read:

> tanto ch'i' vidi de le cose belle
> che porta 'l ciel, per un pertugio tondo.
> E quindi uscimmo a riveder le stelle.
>
> [until at last through a round hole
> I saw the beautiful things that heaven holds.
> And out we went to rebehold the stars.]

PAGE **41** | 'walking along . . . quince orchard'—Jaccottet recalls his prose text 'Blason vert et blanc' (Blazon in Green and White) in *Cahier de verdure* (1990; in *Oeuvres*, pp. 752–59). See 'Notebook of Greenery' in *And, Nonetheless*, pp. 40–57.

PAGE **42** | 'Nah ist . . . gib uns'—from Hölderlin, 'Patmos' in *Sämtliche Gedichte*, pp. 350–60.

PAGE **43** | 'the memory of Saint John'—The legend that Saint John wrote the Book of Revelation on the Greek island of Patmos is based on Revelation 1:9:

> I, John, who am your brother, and compan-
> ion in tribulation, and in the kingdom and
> patience of Jesus Christ, was in the isle that

is called Patmos, for the word of God, and
for the testimony of Jesus Christ.

The Last Book of Madrigals

PAGE 51 | 'lunar pearl . . . the Pleiades'—The constellation
Pleiades is also known as 'The Seven Sisters'. In French,
Jaccottet writes 'boucle' here, literally 'buckle', but perhaps
one also hears 'boucle d'oreille' (earring).

PAGES 54, 55 | 'Le chariot' is one of the names given to the
constellation Ursa Major in French, also known as 'La
Grande Ourse'. In English, some traditions have somewhat
similarly called it 'The Wagon'. The phrase at the end of
the poem, 'the other one', also refers to the constellation.

PAGES 62, 63 | 'Guido, i'vorrei . . . saremmo noi'—Dante's
sonnet is poem LII of *Rime*. The first two lines quoted by
Jaccottet, 'Guido, i' vorrei che tu e Lapo ed io / fossimo presi
per incantamento' ('Guido, I'd like you, Lapo, and me / to
be put under a spell'). Guido Cavalcanti replied with his
sonnet: 'S'io fossi quelli che d'amor fu degno' ('If I were
one of those worthy of love').

PAGE 67 | 'written when Ungaretti was . . . eighty years old'—
Giuseppe Ungaretti's last poem is 'L'impietrito e il velluto'
(The Petrified One and the Velvet). He notes that it was
written between the night of 31 December 1969 and the
morning of 1 January 1970. Here is the context of the image
recalled by Jaccottet:

> Gli scabri messi emersi dall'abisso
> Che recano, dondolo del vuoto,
> Verso l'alambiccare
> Del vecchissimo ossesso
> La eco di strazio dello spento flutto

Durato appena un attimo
Sparito con le sue sinistre barche.

[The coarse messengers who emerged from the
       abyss
And who bear, emptiness in a to-and-fro,
Towards the obsessed old man
Racking his brain,
The anguished echo of the spent billow
That lasted barely a moment
And vanished with its sinister skiffs.]

Jaccottet was the French translator of Ungaretti (1888–1970). See their *Correspondance 1946–1970* (José-Flore Tappy ed.) (Paris: Gallimard, 2008) as well as Jaccottet's translations of Ungaretti's work, *Innocence et mémoire* (Paris: Gallimard, 1969) and *Vie d'un homme: Poésie 1914–1970* (Paris: Gallimard, 1973).

PAGE 83 | 'All the wheat is ablaze . . .'—the poem recalls Jaccottet's prose text 'Sur les degrés montants' (Ascending the Steps) in *Cahier de verdure*. See 'Notebook of Greenery' in *And, Nonetheless*, pp. 58–69.

PAGES 91, 93 | 'between the horns of Lyra'—Jaccottet refers to Lyra and then, in the next poem, to the 'Swan' (or Cygnus); it is possible that he is alluding to mythology associated with the constellations. The brightest star in Lyra is called Vega; the name is borrowed from Latin, 'Wega' or 'Vega', which in turn, according to *Merriam-Webster Dictionary*, has been altered from the terminal syllables of the Arabic 'al-nasr al-wāqi', literally, 'the descending eagle'. Which is why I have translated 'griffes' as 'talon marks' instead of, for instance, 'claw marks'. Moreover, it is said that Orpheus was transformed into the Swan after his death and was placed in the sky next to his lyre, the constellation Lyra. The myth of Leda and the swan is also present here.